I0813860

KID CHEMISTRY LAB

EXPLORING MATTER & PHYSICAL CHANGES

Jessica Rusick

Checkerboard Library

An Imprint of Abdo Publishing
abdobooks.com

ABDOBOOKS.COM

Published by Abdo Publishing, a division of ABDO, PO Box 398166, Minneapolis, Minnesota 55439.

Printed in China
052022
092022

Design and Production: Kelly Doudna, Mighty Media, Inc.
Editor: Liz Salzmann
Cover Photograph: SDI Productions/iStockphoto
Interior Photographs: Andrea Izzotti/Shutterstock Images, p. 21; apiguide/Shutterstock Images, p. 23; Elizaveta Galitckaia/Shutterstock Images, p. 7; Fiona M. Donnelly/Shutterstock Images, p. 15; Jag_cz/Shutterstock Images, p. 17; Lora0212/iStockphoto, p. 25; Mighty Media, Inc., pp. 26, 27, 28, 29; Monkey Business Images/Shutterstock Images, p. 19; RHJPhtotoandilustration/Shutterstock Images, p. 11; The spirit of reality/Shutterstock Images, p. 5; Thorsten Spoerlein/Shutterstock Images, p. 13; Why Design/Shutterstock Images, p. 16; Wikimedia Commons, p. 9

Library of Congress Control Number: 2021953162

Publisher's Cataloging-in-Publication Data
Names: Rusick, Jessica, author.
Title: Exploring matter & physical changes / by Jessica Rusick.
Description: Minneapolis, Minnesota : Abdo Publishing, 2023 | Series: Kid chemistry lab | Includes online resources and index.
Identifiers: ISBN 9781532199004 (lib. bdg.) | ISBN 9781098272937 (ebook)
Subjects: LCSH: Chemistry--Juvenile literature. | Matter--Juvenile literature. | Change--Juvenile literature. | Science projects--Juvenile literature.
Classification: DDC 540--dc23

CONTENTS

Chapter 1

WHAT IS MATTER?

Matter is anything that takes up physical space. It makes up everything around us! You are made of matter. So are the food you eat and the air you breathe.

Matter can't be created or destroyed. It can only change form. Matter can change in physical or chemical ways. A physical change affects what a substance looks like. It doesn't change what the substance is. A chemical change transforms substances into different substances.

Crumpling a sheet of paper is a physical change. The paper's shape is different, but it is still paper. Burning paper is a chemical change. Fire transforms the paper into ash and smoke. These are new substances.

Matter doesn't just exist on Earth. Objects in outer space, such as the moon, are made of matter too.

Chapter 2

MATTER BASICS

All matter is made of small bits called atoms. Scientists have identified 118 types of atoms, one for each known element. An element is a substance that can't be broken down into different substances. Oxygen is an element. So is gold.

Atoms can combine in millions of different ways. This makes new substances called compounds. Salt is a compound. It is made of **sodium** and **chlorine** atoms. Matter is often a mixture of many elements and compounds.

Chemistry is the study of matter. Chemists study what matter is made of and how it interacts with other matter. Understanding matter helps chemists understand the world.

Atoms are too small to see with regular microscopes. Scientists use special electron microscopes to study them.

Chapter 3

ATOMIC THEORY

Humans have studied matter for thousands of years. The ancient Greek philosopher Democritus believed all matter could be broken down into small units. He called these pieces *atomos*. But few people paid attention to his ideas at the time.

In 1789, French chemist Antoine-Laurent Lavoisier proposed the law of conservation of mass. This law states that matter cannot be created or destroyed. In the early 1800s, British scientist John Dalton built on this idea when he developed the atomic theory of matter. It states that all matter is made of atoms.

Dalton's theory was a scientific **breakthrough**. It helped chemists better understand and study matter. Over the years, Dalton's atomic theory has been expanded on by other chemists.

John Dalton

Chapter 4

PROPERTIES OF MATTER

All matter has physical properties. Picture an object. What shape is it? What color is it? Shape and color are some of the object's physical properties.

Volume, mass, and density are other important physical properties of matter. Volume is the amount of space something takes up. Mass is how much matter something contains.

Density is the amount of mass compared to volume. Imagine two boxes that are the same size. The first contains ten marbles. The second contains 1,000 marbles. The second box has a higher density because it has more mass filling up the volume.

Hardness is a physical property. The hardest natural substance is diamond.

Some physical **properties** are extensive. This means they change based on how much matter there is. A small piece of gold will have less mass than a large piece of gold. The small piece is also probably shorter than the large piece. So, mass and length are extensive properties.

Other physical properties are intensive. This means they are always the same regardless of the amount of matter. Gold, for example, is **malleable**. This means it can easily be flattened into sheets. A small piece of gold is just as malleable as a large piece. So, malleability is an intensive property. Other intensive properties include color and density.

Matter also has chemical properties. These properties indicate whether and how matter will undergo chemical change. Flammability is a chemical property. It indicates how easily a substance burns.

Toxicity is a chemical property that indicates how poisonous something is. The skin of golden poison frogs is coated with one of the most toxic substances in the world.

Chapter 5

STATES OF MATTER

State is another physical **property** of matter. The three main states of matter are solid, liquid, and gas. Some matter is solid. In a solid, atoms are packed tightly together. They do not move, and they are always in contact with each other. This gives solids a rigid shape.

There are two types of solids. Crystalline solids have atoms that repeat in an organized structure. Diamond is crystalline. Other solids are amorphous. They have an **irregular** structure with no repeating pattern. Glass and rubber are amorphous solids.

In a liquid, atoms are not as closely packed as in a solid. The atoms are always in contact with each other. But unlike in a solid, they can move around. This means liquids do not have a constant shape. A liquid will take the shape of the container it is in.

Snowflakes are crystalline solids.

Atoms in a gas are far apart from each other. They move in many directions. Like liquids, gases do not have shapes. They fill whatever container they're in.

There is a fourth state of matter called plasma. It is a type of gas. Plasma exists naturally mostly in Earth's atmosphere and in outer space. For example, stars and lightning contain plasma. Scientists can also create plasma in laboratories. It has been used to make screens for computers and televisions.

= atom

GAS

LIQUID

SOLID

The aurora borealis is created by plasma from the sun.

Chapter 6

CHANGING MATTER

Matter's properties can change. A physical change can be a change in state, shape, volume, or any other physical property. Mixing food coloring into water is a physical change. So is heating a pan or chopping down a tree. Other physical changes include melting, crushing, and tearing.

Physical changes are sometimes possible to reverse. If you mix peanuts and chocolate chips together, you can easily separate them. However, not all physical changes are possible to reverse. If you cut your hair, you can't reattach the pieces you cut off.

Physical changes are often caused by a force, such as pressure. Forming clay into a different shape is a physical change. 

Chemical changes cannot be reversed without another chemical reaction. Often, they are impossible to reverse at all. Baking batter into cake, for example, is a chemical change. It's impossible to turn the cake back into batter.

It can sometimes be difficult to tell whether a change is chemical or physical. A color change can signal a physical change. But it can signal a chemical change as well! Iron, for example, is usually gray or silver. Rusty iron is orange. Is rusting a chemical or physical change?

The best way to determine the type of change is to **analyze** the chemicals present before and after. Chemical changes make new chemical substances. Physical changes do not. The orange rust is a new substance called iron oxide. It develops when iron is exposed to oxygen and water. So, rusting is a chemical change.

The Statue of Liberty is made of copper. Over time, the copper has reacted with elements in the air. This causes a chemical change turning the copper a blue-green color.

Chapter 7

PHASE CHANGES

Another type of physical change is a phase change. A phase change is when matter turns from one state to another. Melting changes matter from solid to liquid. Freezing changes liquid into a solid. Vaporizing, or boiling, changes a liquid into a gas.

Other phase changes are condensation, sublimation, and deposition. Condensation changes a gas into a liquid. Sublimation changes a solid to a gas. Deposition changes a gas into a solid.

Phase changes happen when heat is added or taken away. For example, water freezes into ice at 32 degrees Fahrenheit (0°C). This is water's freezing point. Water becomes water vapor, or gas, at 212 degrees Fahrenheit (100°C). This is water's boiling point. Substances can have different freezing and boiling points.

Condensation causes water to form on the outside of a glass of ice water. The cold water cools water vapor in the air touching the glass. The vapor changes to liquid and sticks to the glass.

Phase changes are endothermic or exothermic. Heat is added in an endothermic reaction. In an exothermic reaction, heat is taken away. So, melting is an endothermic reaction. Freezing is an exothermic reaction.

Phase changes might seem like chemical changes. Ice, for example, may look like a new and different substance than water. But ice and water are chemically the same. They are both made of the same number and types of atoms. The only difference is how the atoms are arranged in each substance.

White frost forms through deposition. Water vapor in the air freezes directly into ice. It doesn't change to water first.

OOZING OOBLECK

WHAT HAPPENS

Oobleck has **properties** of both a solid and a liquid. Oobleck is called a non-Newtonian **fluid**. Quickly tapping or hitting the oobleck pushes the cornstarch particles closer together. This makes the oobleck feel solid. If you move more slowly, the cornstarch particles flow out of the way. This makes the oobleck feel like liquid.

EXPERIMENT!

What happens if you place different objects in the oobleck? Do they sink or float? Why do you think this is?

MATERIALS

- water
- measuring cups
- large bowl
- cornstarch

STEPS

1 Pour 1 cup of water into a large bowl.

2 Add 1½ cups of cornstarch. Mix it with your hands. Add more cornstarch until the mixture is gooey. You have made oobleck!

3 Tap the oobleck with your hand. What happens? Does the oobleck behave like a solid or a liquid?

4 Press down gently on the oobleck. Does the oobleck behave like solid or a liquid?

5 Wash your hands after handling the oobleck. When you're done experimenting, put the oobleck in the trash. Do not put oobleck down the drain.

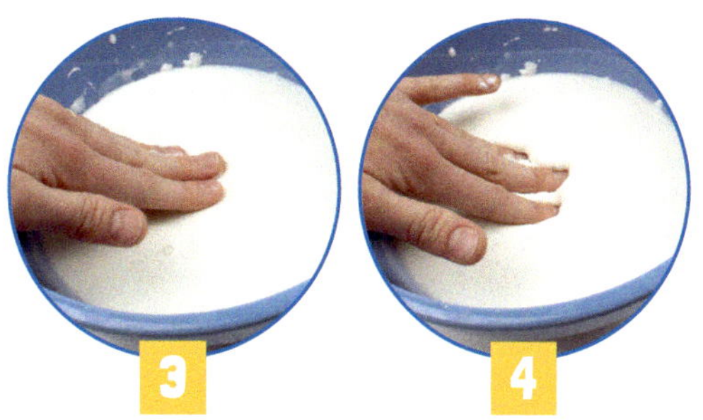

THE SCIENTIFIC METHOD

Want to experiment like a real chemist? Follow the scientific method! The scientific method is a process scientists use to answer questions.

1. Ask a question. Research your question to learn more about it.
2. Develop a **hypothesis**. This is your best guess about the answer to your question.
3. Experiment to test your hypothesis. Record what happens during the experiment.
4. Review the results of your experiment to draw a conclusion. Was your hypothesis supported? Why or why not? Share your results with others.

DENSITY COLUMN

WHAT HAPPENS

Density is a physical **property**. Each liquid has a different density. Less dense liquids float on top of denser liquids in separate layers. Denser liquids sink to the bottom. Honey, maple syrup, and corn syrup are among the densest liquids. Dish soap is denser than milk, and both are denser than water. Oils are less dense than water.

MATERIALS

- 4 plastic cups
- marker
- 4 liquids that vary in thickness (see Suggested Liquids list for ideas)
- food coloring
- pencil
- paper
- clear glass jar

Suggested Liquids

corn syrup
dish soap
honey
maple syrup
milk
vegetable oil
water

STEPS

1 Label each cup with the name of a liquid. Pour some of each liquid into its cup. Add food coloring to any uncolored liquids.

2 Guess which liquids are the densest and which are the least dense. Record your guesses.

3 Slowly and carefully pour the liquid you think is densest into the jar. Wait for the liquid to settle.

4 Repeat step 3 with the remaining liquids in order of density.

5 What does the jar look like? Do you think you guessed the liquids' densities correctly? Why or why not?

EXPERIMENT!

What happens if you pour the liquids into the jar in a different order? Do they still form separate layers? Do any mix together?

GLOSSARY

analyze—to examine something to find out what it is or what makes it work.

breakthrough—an important discovery that happens after trying for a long time to understand or do something.

chlorine—a chemical element that under normal conditions is a greenish-yellow gas and has a strong smell.

fluid—a substance that flows or takes the shape of its container. A liquid or a gas is a fluid.

hypothesis (hye-PAH-thi-sis)—an unproven idea or theory based on known facts that leads to further study.

irregular—not evenly or uniformly shaped, arranged, or spaced.

malleable—capable of being pressed, stretched, or bent into different shapes.

property—a special quality or feature of something.

sodium—a soft, waxy, silver-white chemical element. It is found in compounds such as salt and baking soda.

ONLINE RESOURCES

To learn more about matter, please visit **abdobooklinks.com** or scan this QR code. These links are routinely monitored and updated to provide the most current information available.

INDEX